ws

PICTURE A COUNTRY

India

Henry Pluckrose

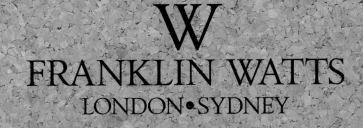

FRANKLIN WATTS
LONDON·SYDNEY

This is the Indian flag.

First Published in 1998
by Franklin Watts
This edition 2001

Franklin Watts
96 Leonard Street
London EC2A 4XD

Franklin Watts Australia
56 O'Riordan Street
Alexandria, Sydney
NSW 2015

© Franklin Watts 1998

ISBN 0 7496 4281 5

A CIP catalogue record for this book is
available from the British Library

Dewey Decimal Classification Number:915.4

10 9 8 7 6 5 4 3 2 1

Series Editor: Rachel Cooke
Designer: Kirstie Billingham
Picture research: Juliet Duff

Printed in Great Britain

Photographic acknowledgements:

Cover: Top The Hutchison Library, bottom left Getty
Images (Alan Smith), bottom right Robert Harding
Picture Library.

AA Photo Library p. 14;
Stephani Colasanti p. 10;
Colorific p. 20 (Raghubir Singh);
Getty Images pp. 8 (Chris Noble), 11 (Julian Calder),
13 (Anthony Cassidy), 22 (Paul Harris), 26 (Alan Smith),
29 (Manoj Shah);
Robert Harding Picture Library pp. 12 (James Strachan),
15 (Adina Tovy), 16, 24 (J. H. C. Wilson);
The Hutchison Library pp. 19, 28;
Images of India pp. 9 (Dinodia Picture Agency),
25 (Nick Withey), 27 (Dinodia Picture Agency);
Impact Photos p. 18 (Mark Henley)
Link Picture Library pp. 17 (Orde Eliason),
21 (Chandra Kishore Prasad).
All other photography by Steve Shott.

Map by Julian Baker.

With thanks to Arvind, Dipika and Gemini Patel

Contents

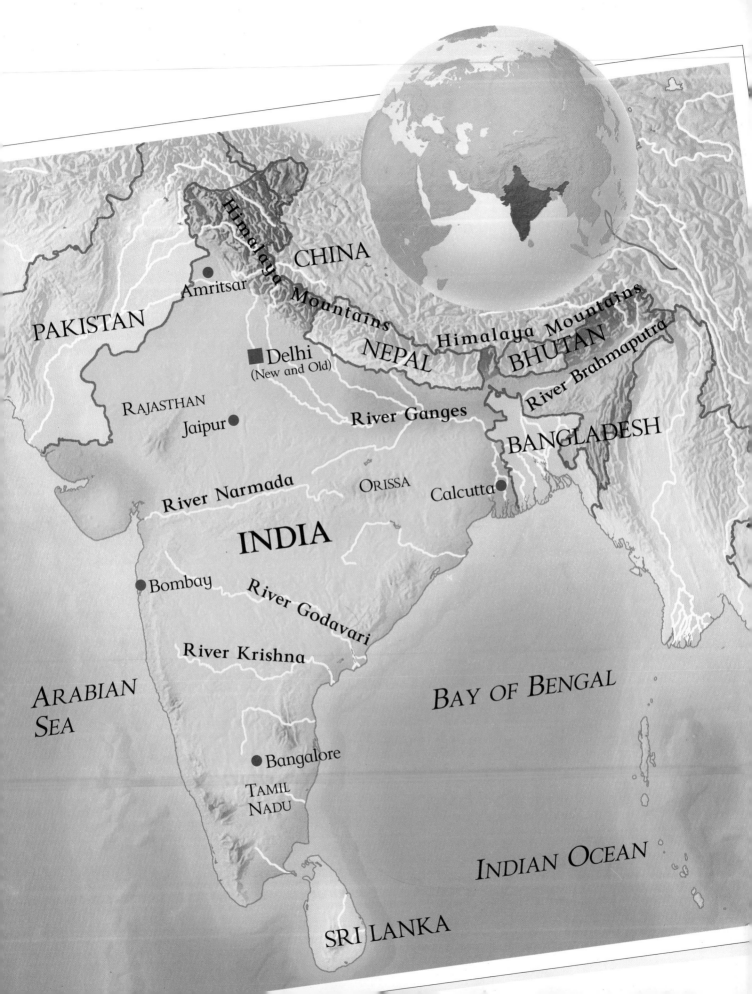

Where is India?

This is a map of India.
India is in Asia.
India is the seventh largest country in the world.

Here are some Indian stamps and money.

Indian money is counted in rupees.

The Indian landscape

India is a country of high mountains, great rivers, plains and deserts.

Summer in India begins in March and ends in May. The weather is dry and hot.

Summer is followed by four months of rainy weather. These rains are called monsoons. Winter begins in November.

This camel is in a desert in Rajasthan, a region of north-west India.

This village is on the edge of the Himalayas in northern India. The Himalayas are the highest mountains in the world.

The Indian people

People first built towns and cities
in India over 5,000 years ago.
Today nearly 1,000 million people
live in India.

These crowds are at a festival in Bombay.

The Sikhs first built the Golden Temple in Amritsar about 400 years ago. They believe the pool beside it is sacred.

Many different peoples live in India.
The Sikhs are one of India's many peoples.

Many languages are spoken in India, too.
The most important language is Hindi.

This is a busy street in Calcutta.

Where they live

Most Indians live and work
in the countryside.

There are some large cities.
Calcutta is India's largest city.
Over 10 million people live there.

The capital city

New Delhi has many modern office blocks.

New Delhi is the capital of India.
It is called "New" because it was built near
to a much older city with the same name.

The Red Fort in the old town of Delhi was built by Shah Jehan, who ruled northern India from 1628 to 1658.

Indian factories

Indian factories make all sorts of goods.
In the city of Bombay, cotton is woven
and made into clothing.
Other goods are still made by hand.

This man is making parts that will go inside a computer.

The city of Bangalore is a "computer" town.
It has many factories which make computers.
These computers are sold all over the world.

Farming

Indian farmers grow many kinds of food - wheat, coffee, tea, sugar, rice and fruit. They also grow trees which give us rubber, and the plants which give us cotton.

This woman is planting rice in a paddy field in the Orissa region of eastern India.

Women pick the tea leaves by hand.
The leaves will be dried and sold to make tea.

The picture above shows workers
on a farm where they grow tea.
The farm is in Tamil Nadu,
a region famous for its tea.

Family life

This Indian family are having a day out.
The woman is wearing a sari.

Some Indian children go to school.
Others have to work to earn money
for their families.

These men are making sweet fritters called *jalebis*.
They are selling them in a market in Jaipur.

Indian food

An Indian meal is made up of many different foods. There are nearly always vegetables with rice or bread.

There may also be soup, fish and meat, cheese and yogurt, milk and coconut cakes, and sweets made of almonds and syrup.

This is a selection of Indian foods. Some of them have been flavoured with spices.

Out and about

Indians enjoy going to the cinema.
A lot of Indian films are made in Bombay -
it is sometimes called Bollywood!

These posters in Bombay are advertising Indian films.

Cricket matches are played on the fields
in front of the university in Bombay.

Cricket and hockey are popular sports in India.
Some Indians also play polo.
Polo is an Indian game. It is played
on horseback with sticks and a ball.

This Hindu temple called Laxmi Narayan is in Delhi.

Temples and festivals

India is a land of temples. Temples are places where people go to worship.

The Indian people follow many different religions, including Hinduism, Islam and Sikhism. Most Indians are Hindu.

One important Hindu festival is Diwali. Diwali, the festival of light, takes place in October or November. It marks the beginning of the Hindu New Year.

Hindus celebrate Diwali by lighting candles.

Visiting India

If you go to India, you might visit a wildlife park and see elephants, rhinoceroses, monkeys or even a tiger.

You might also watch Indian dancers or visit India's beautiful buildings.

Index

About this book

The last decade of the 20th century has been marked by an explosion in communications technology. The effect of this revolution upon the young child should not be underestimated. The television set brings a cascade of ever-changing images from around the world into the home, but the information presented is only on the screen for a few moments before the programme moves on to consider some other issue.

Instant pictures, instant information do not easily satisfy young children's emotional and intellectual needs. Young children take time to assimilate knowledge, to relate what they already know to ideas and information which are new.

The books in this series seek to provide snapshots of everyday life in countries in different parts of the world. The images have been selected to encourage the young reader to look, to question, to talk. Unlike the TV picture, each page can be studied for as long as is necessary and subsequently returned to as a point of reference. For example, an Indian child's daily life might be compared with their own; a discussion might develop about the ways in which food is prepared and eaten in a country whose culture and customs are different from their own.

The comparison of similarity and difference is the recurring theme in each of the titles in this series. People in different lands are superficially different. Where they live (the climate and terrain) obviously shapes the sort of houses that are built, but people across the world need shelter; coins may look different, but in each country people use money.

At a time when the world seems to be shrinking, it is important for children to be given the opportunity to focus upon those things which are common to all the peoples of the world. By exploring the themes touched upon in the book, children will begin to appreciate that there are strands in the everyday life of human beings which are universal.